OLYMPICS

GLOBAL CITIZENS: SPORTS

Published in the United States of America by Cherry Lake Publishing
Ann Arbor, Michigan
www.cherrylakepublishing.com

Content Adviser: Liv Williams, Editor, www.iLivExtreme.com
Reading Adviser: Marla Conn, MS, Ed., Literacy specialist, Read-Ability, Inc.

Photo Credits: ©Paul Bradbury/iStock, cover, 1; ©Konstantinos Ouzounidis/iStock, 5; ©evgenii mitroshin/
Shutterstock, 6; ©North Wind Picture Archives, 7; ©Leonard Zhukovsky/Shutterstock, 8, 13; ©Petr Toman/
Shutterstock, 10; ©Rkaphotography/Dreamstime, 15; ©Alexander Khitrov/Shutterstock, 16; ©World History
Archive/Alamy Stock Photo, 19; ©Sam DCruz/Shutterstock, 22; ©Martynova Anna/Shutterstock, 25;
©Antonio Scorza/Shutterstock, 26; ©Morfeo86ts/Dreamstime, 28

Library of Congress Cataloging-in-Publication Data

Names: Hellebuyck, Adam, author. | Deimel, Laura, author.
Title: Olympics / written by Adam Hellebuyck and Laura Deimel.
Description: Ann Arbor, Michigan : Cherry Lake Publishing, [2019] | Series: Global Citizens: Sports |
    Audience: Grades 4 to 6 | Includes bibliographical references and index.
Identifiers: LCCN 2019004213 | ISBN 9781534147539 (hardcover) | ISBN 9781534150393 (paperback) |
    ISBN 9781534148963 (pdf) | ISBN 9781534151826 (hosted ebook)
Subjects: LCSH: Olympics—Juvenile literature.
Classification: LCC GV721.53 .H45 2019 | DDC 796.48—dc23
LC record available at https://lccn.loc.gov/2019004213

Cherry Lake Publishing would like to acknowledge the work of the Partnership for 21st Century Learning.
Please visit *www.p21.org* for more information.

Printed in the United States of America
Corporate Graphics

ABOUT THE AUTHORS

Laura Deimel is a fourth grade teacher and Adam Hellebuyck is a high school social studies
teacher at University Liggett School in Grosse Pointe Woods, Michigan. They have worked
together for the past 8 years and are thrilled they could combine two of their passions, reading
and sports, into this work.

TABLE OF CONTENTS

CHAPTER 1

History: It Started with Zeus

The Olympic Games have a long history, dating back to ancient times. In fact, the Games have been bringing people together for almost 1,200 years!

A Religious Ceremony

Historians believe that the Olympic Games began in 776 BCE to honor the Greek gods. The Games were first held on the plains of Olympia in Greece. Ancient Greeks believed the gods lived on top of Mount Olympus, which was near Olympia.

The early Olympic Games were a religious **ceremony** that honored Zeus, the god of gods. The Games were also a way for Greek cities to come together. These cities, which were often at

While women weren't allowed to compete in the ancient Olympics, they did have a separate festival called the Heraean Games.

war with each other, would make an "Olympic **truce**." This truce forced all Greek cities to stop fighting each other during the Games.

The Games were first held on a single day, but were later expanded to 5 days and reoccurred every 4 years. In these early Games, people competed in many different events. There were athletic competitions like running, long jumping, boxing, and wrestling. There were also competitions in music, public speaking, and theater!

The five interlocking ring colors and the original white backdrop of the Olympic symbol represent the continents and different national flags around the world.

The Modern Games

The Olympics were held regularly until around the 5th century CE. Many claim that Christian Roman Emperor Theodosius I put an end to the Games. Other historians found evidence that the Games probably stopped because no one was able to afford them anymore.

The youngest modern Olympian to compete was Dimitrios Loundras. He was only 10 years old when he competed in the 1896 Games in gymnastics.

The Olympic gold medal is actually made of more silver than gold!
It contains at least 92.5 percent silver.

The Games were not held for the next 1,500 years until Pierre de Coubertin, a French nobleman, proposed to restart the Olympic Games without the religious ties. He thought the Olympics could help people focus on building a healthy mind and body. This Olympic revival was held in 1896 in Athens, Greece. Thirteen countries competed in nine different events like gymnastics, lawn tennis, and swimming. While these Olympic Games were a success, no one expected that they would be held regularly like the ancient games. Yet, the Olympics were held every 4 years and slowly became more popular each time they were held. They have been held every 4 years since 1896, except during World Wars I and II.

Women in the Olympics

Women have participated in the Olympic Games since 1900. That year, 22 women out of a total of 997 athletes participated. They competed in two events: tennis and golf. Women competed in every Olympic sport for the first time in the 2012 Olympic Games in London.

After a 112-year absence from the Games, golf was added back temporarily. It was included in the 2016 Games and will be an event during the 2020 Games in Tokyo, Japan.

The Games Change

The types of events featured in the Olympics have greatly changed since 1896. There are no longer music or theater events, but there are many new sporting events. New sports are usually added when they become popular around the world. For example, basketball was added to the Olympic Games in 1936. Skateboarding, surfing, and climbing will be added to the Olympic **roster** in 2020!

Developing Questions

The competitive events at the Olympics have changed over time. Using reliable sources on the internet, create a list of sports that have been added or removed from the Olympic Games since 1996. After completing your list, think about why new sports were added. Think also about why some sports were removed. What questions do you think experts ask before they add a new sport to the Olympics? Are these the same questions experts would ask when they think about removing a sport? If you were to add a new sport to the Olympics, what would it be and why?

Geography: A United World

The location of the Olympic Games has always been important. While the ancient Games were always held on the plains of Olympia, Greece, the modern event travels around the world. Since their revival in 1896, the Games have moved from country to country every 4 years. The International Olympic Committee, the group that helps to plan the Olympics, decides which cities will host the Games. Until 1964, all Olympic Games were held in either North America or Europe. That year, the Games were held in Tokyo, Japan. The most recent Olympic Games were held in Rio de Janeiro, Brazil, in 2016.

In Olympic history, the United States has won the most medals, with 2,827 medals as of 2018.

The Olympic Games in Europe

Europe has hosted the most Summer and Winter Olympics: 32 of the 51 Games since 1896. The most recent Summer Olympics in Europe were held in London in 2012. Almost 11,000 athletes competed! London has hosted the Olympic Games three times since 1896.

Paris, France, has hosted the Olympic Games twice since 1896. It will host again in 2024, for the Summer Olympic Games. That will make Paris the second city in the world to host the Games three times. While many other cities have built brand-new arenas for the events, Paris plans to **renovate** many of the stadiums in the city instead.

The Olympic Games in Asia

Including the Tokyo Games in 1964, 8 of the 51 Olympic Games have been hosted in Asia. The 1964 Games were also **groundbreaking** because they were the first to be shown live worldwide on television. Tokyo will host the Summer Olympics again in 2020 and Beijing in 2022.

Watchdog Agencies

When the modern Olympics began, only summer sports were included in the competitions. But the Olympic Committee soon wanted people to also compete in winter sports. On January 25, 1924, the first Winter Olympics were held in Chamonix, France. There were 258 athletes (247 men and 11 women) from 16 countries. The athletes competed in 18 events, which included bobsledding, figure skating, curling, and ice hockey.

Until 1992, the Summer and Winter Olympic Games were considered one large event and were held in the same year. After that year, the Games were split into separate events held in different years. Today, they are held 2 years apart.

The 2012 London Olympics was the first time all participating countries sent women to compete in the events.

PyeongChang, South Korea, is the smallest city to host the Olympics since Lillehammer, Norway, in 1994.

The 2018 Winter Olympics were held in PyeongChang, South Korea. During these games, North Korea and South Korea, which are rival countries, decided to march into the opening ceremonies together. Both countries wanted to show that they had a goal of **resolving** their differences by working together at the Olympic Games.

Olympics on Other Continents

Other continents have also hosted the Olympics. North America has hosted the Summer and Winter Olympics 12 times (in Canada, Mexico, and the United States). Two of the Games have been hosted in Oceania, which is made up of the islands in the southern Pacific Ocean. These Games were held in Australia. South America has hosted the Games once, in Rio de Janeiro in 2016.

Gathering and Evaluating Sources

Currently, Africa and Antarctica are the only continents to have never hosted any Olympic Games. Why do you think this is? Research the geographic and economic features of these two continents. Compare these features to those of the other continents. If you were on the Olympic Committee, what features would be important to you? Are geographical terrain and weather important factors? Would you want a country that needs to build venues from the ground up? Or would you rather the country have venues that would only need to be renovated or expanded?

CHAPTER 3

Civics: Standing Up for What's Right

The Olympics also help address problems around the world. Athletes and countries have used different ways to solve these issues since the Olympic Games began.

Taking a Stand at the Games

In 1968, the winners of the 200-meter dash wanted people to think about **civil rights** in the United States. The gold medalist, Tommie Smith, and the bronze medalist, John Carlos, wanted to show that they were frustrated with how black Americans were being treated in the United States at the time. When they received their medals, they raised their fists in the air while the national anthem played, to show that frustration. While many people at the time were upset with Smith and Carlos, the two have been

Many Olympic athletes over the years have stood up for what they believe in.

honored with many awards for their actions. In 2008, they received the Arthur Ashe Courage Award at the ESPY (Excellence in Sports Performance Yearly) Awards.

Rule 50

The International Olympic Committee has rules for athletes who want to protest a problem. Rule 50 in the Olympic **Charter** states that an athlete isn't allowed to protest at any Olympic stadium or official event. While it is against the rules to protest, sometimes the rule isn't **enforced**.

In 2016, the United States Olympic Committee took a stand on this rule. Scott Blackmun, the committee leader, said that the committee supported Olympic athletes and their right to express themselves at the Games. The committee also invited Smith and Carlos to come to the White House with the 2016 Olympic team to meet President Barack Obama

The Olympic Games are also about bringing together people
from all over the world and setting aside differences.

While there weren't any boycotts during the 2008 Beijing Games in China, there were many people who protested against China hosting.

Conflicts Between Countries

Sometimes countries do not send athletes to the Olympic Games because they disagree with something that the host country has done. This is called a **boycott**. This has happened seven times in the history of the Olympic Games. The first boycott happened at the 1936 Games held in Berlin, Germany. The **Nazis** were in power at the time. Spain and the Soviet Union boycotted the Games.

During the **Cold War**, the United States and the Soviet Union boycotted the Olympic Games in each other's countries. The most recent boycott occurred in 1988, when seven countries did not send athletes to the Games in South Korea. There have been no boycotts since then.

Developing Claims and Using Evidence

While the Olympic Games are about friendly athletic competition between countries, they can be used to make people understand some of the problems that those countries or the world have right now. Think about what is important to you. If you were an Olympic athlete, is there anything you would want people around the world to think about or take action on? If so, how would you share your thoughts respectfully with the rest of the world? Research other protests that happened during the Olympic Games. Were they respectful? Why or why not?

CHAPTER 4

Economics: Buildings and Mascots

The Olympic Games cost a lot of money to host. Countries need to build new arenas for sports competitions, build **lodging** for athletes and fans, and make improvements to their cities. Let's take a closer look.

Building Buildings

Experts believe that the 2016 Summer Olympics in Rio de Janeiro cost over $13 billion to hold! Why did this event cost so much?

Rio de Janeiro built nine new arenas to hold events for the Games. The city also renovated 11 other stadiums around the city. To make it easier for athletes and fans to reach the stadiums,

As of 2019, the 2014 Winter Olympics held in Sochi, Russia, was the most expensive—costing about $51 billion!

Brazil had promised to clean up the heavily polluted Guanabara Bay, the site of the sailing events, before the 2016 Games. But the organizers failed to keep that promise.

the city even built new subway lines! Building the subway alone cost almost $3 billion. Some government officials worried that the new arenas and transportation systems wouldn't be put to use after the Olympics.

They were right to worry, as many previous Olympic venues were deserted not long after the event ended. For example, Atlanta, Georgia, hosted the 1996 Summer Olympics. The city built a $22-million tennis center that sat about 12,000 people.

Afterward, the facility eventually became so neglected that the city now plans on demolishing the venue.

While many cities hosting the Olympic Games only had to improve their **infrastructure**, Rio de Janeiro also had to spend a lot of money to clean up the pollution in and around the city before hosting. The city focused on cleaning up Guanabara Bay, where the sailing and windsurfing events were held. Experts believe this cleanup cost over $1 billion. However, many claim it still wasn't enough.

Taking Informed Action

*Think more about **mascots** and how they can help to represent an idea or a group of people. Is there a group or a charity in your town that you know something about or like being a part of? Do they have a mascot? If they have a mascot, what does it show about the group? If they do not have a mascot, would they benefit from having one? Make a list of different organizations and companies that have mascots and another list of ones that don't. Why do you think some have mascots and others don't?*

According to the designers, Wenlock and Mandeville symbolize
the United Kingdom's Industrial Revolution.

Mascots of the Olympics

Every Olympics has a mascot. These mascots connect children to the events. They give children a friendly character to help them better understand the spirit of the Olympic Games and the culture of the host country.

The Olympic Games have had mascots since 1968—but they aren't always big sellers. The mascots of the 2012 London Games were Wenlock and Mandeville. The beloved British toy manufacturer Hornby created special products based on these mascots, expecting to sell out, only to have the opposite happen. The company reported it lost about $4.2 million that year. The year prior to the Games, the company had actually made a $5 million **profit**. Many people blamed the strange-looking mascots for the loss.

Communicating Conclusions

Based on everything you learned about the Olympic Games, did you know the importance of the Olympic mascots? If your city were to host the next Games, how would you incorporate the spirit of friendly competition into your mascot design? How would you represent your own community and its culture and history in a design? Brainstorm a few ideas with a friend or family member. What designs did you come up with for your mascot?

Think About It

Since the modern Olympic Games began in 1896, nearly 30,000 medals have been given to the first-, second-, and third-place competitors in each sport. Some countries have won many more medals than others. The top 10 countries that have won the most medals in the Summer Olympics are listed below. Take a careful look at the data in the chart. Using information from your local library and the internet, try to figure out what has helped these 10 countries win more medals than other countries. Also, think about why the top three countries on the list have been able to win so many more medals than the rest of the top 10! Can you figure out their championship secrets?

Country	Olympic Medals
United States	2,520
Russia	1,865
Germany	1,681
Great Britain	847
France	713
Italy	577
China	543
Australia	497
Sweden	494
Hungary	491

For More Information

Further Reading

Fullman, Joe. *The Olympics: Ancient to Modern*. London: Wayland, 2017.

Gitlin, Marty. *The 1980 U.S. Olympic Boycott*. Ann Arbor, MI: Cherry Lake Publishing, 2014.

Websites

International Olympic Committee
https://www.olympic.org
Visit the official Olympics website to learn more about the Games and their history.

National Geographic Kids—Let the Games Begin: The First Olympics
https://kids.nationalgeographic.com/explore/history/first-olympics
Learn more facts about the first Olympic Games in ancient Greece.

GLOSSARY

boycott (BOI-kaht) joining with others in refusing to deal with someone (as a person, organization, or country) as a way of protesting or forcing changes

ceremony (SER-uh-moh-nee) event with specific rules that honors someone or something

charter (CHAHR-tur) a written set of rules that organizes a group

civil rights (SIV-uhl RITES) the rights that every person should have regardless of his or her sex, race, or religion

Cold War (KOHLD WOR) the nonviolent disagreement between the United States and the Soviet Union, which is now 15 independent states and countries

enforced (en-FORSD) to make people follow a rule or a law

groundbreaking (GROUND-brayk-ing) something never done before

infrastructure (IN-fruh-struk-chur) the basic things that help make a city run, like roads and power lines

lodging (LAHJ-ing) places where a visitor or a tourist can stay the night

mascots (MAS-kahtz) things that are used to represent a group or an event

Nazis (NAHT-seez) people who were part of a political party that controlled Germany from 1933 to 1945 under Adolf Hitler

profit (PRAH-fit) the gain after all the expenses are subtracted from the total amount received

renovate (REN-uh-vate) to fix up something old

resolving (rih-ZAHLV-ing) finding a solution

roster (RAH-stur) a list of the people or things that belong to a particular group or team

truce (TROOS) an agreement between enemies or opponents to stop fighting for a certain period of time

INDEX